UNEXPECTED

UNEXPECTED

UNEXPECTED

LEAVE FEAR BEHIND, MOVE FORWARD
IN FAITH, EMBRACE THE ADVENTURE

STUDY GUIDE

FIVE SESSIONS

CHRISTINE CAINE

WRITTEN BY KEVIN AND SHERRY HARNEY

ZONDERVAN®

ZONDERVAN

Unexpected Study Guide
Copyright © 2018 by Christine Caine

This title is also available as a Zondervan ebook.

Requests for information should be addressed to:
Zondervan, *3900 Sparks Dr. SE, Grand Rapids, Michigan 49546*

ISBN 978-0-310-08930-8

Cover photography: Nate Griffin / @kanakanate
Interior design: Kait Lamphere

First Printing May 2018 / Printed in the United States of America

CONTENTS

OF NOTE

The quotations interspersed throughout this study guide and the introductory comments are excerpts from the book *Unexpected* and the video curriculum of the same name by Christine Caine. All other resources, including the small group questions, session introductions, and between-sessions materials, have been written by Kevin and Sherry Harney in collaboration with Christine Caine.

A WORD FROM
CHRISTINE CAINE

Life is full of surprises, both good and bad. It can be full of unexpected twists and turns that we never saw coming. We can go from hearing a shocking diagnosis to welcoming our first grandchild. From having a rough day at the office to accepting a marriage proposal that evening. From facing an unexpected car repair to being offered a promotion. From planning a vacation to losing everything because of a hurricane.

The unexpected is one of the mysteries of life—something we have no control over but are guaranteed to experience almost every single day of our life.

None of us minds experiencing the unexpected when it's happy or inconsequential. But when the unexpected strikes fear in our hearts or is deeply painful it can throw us into such an emotional state that we find ourselves withdrawing from life and the people we love. In severe cases we even find ourselves stuck . . . unable to move forward.

In this five-session study you will hear God's tender invitation to accept his gracious call to trust him more—in the face of your pain. To move into a deeper intimacy with him than you have ever known—and let him heal your heart. To develop relentless faith so that the next time life throws you a curve ball—which life most certainly will—you will be able to navigate your way through, still living the adventure he planned for you. And maybe even living a version of the adventure that's beyond what you could have ever imagined.

It's possible to learn how to live with a faith that is so confident in God, it can't be shaken—even when the ground underneath is giving way. That's what Abraham did. God extended to him the same invitation he extends to us—to trust with all his heart—and Abraham said yes—even though he had no idea where his *yes* would lead. He left the expected and stepped into the unexpected. He didn't know where he was going, who he would meet, or what it would cost. He didn't know any of the pain that might lie ahead. But he knew God would be with him. He knew God would guide him, protect him, and provide for him—and he refused to be shaken: "By faith Abraham, when called to go to a place he would later receive as his inheritance, obeyed and went, *even though he did not know where he was going*" (Hebrews 11:8, emphasis added).

I believe we can live this expectantly. This hopefully. This freely. This faith-filled. In the face of *everything* that comes our way. Even in the face of the unexpected that invades our lives. Even in the unpredictable times in which we live. Even with all the chaos happening around the world.

I have no doubt you are part of this study because God has a life of adventure planned for you. I know he created us all on purpose, for a purpose—and he never wants fear of the unexpected or from the unexpected to hold us back. So, as you take part in this five-session study, as you allow the Holy Spirit to light your path, let's go together. Let's leave fear behind, move forward in faith, and embrace the adventure.

With you on the glorious and unexpected journey of faith,
Christine Caine

EXPECT THE UNEXPECTED

INTRODUCTION

Kirk and Ashleigh were in their late twenties and already knew the heartbreak of bad news. After three years of tests, procedures, and tears, they sat with the doctor as he explained that they would not be able to conceive. They had reached the end of their medical options. They would have to adjust their expectations. Eight months later they were in the same doctor's office. Ashleigh had been sick for almost a month and the doctor sat them down with unexpected news. "I don't know how to explain this, but you are pregnant. You are three months along. Congratulations!" They did not see this coming.

Hank thanked all the guests for coming: family, friends, and work associates. As he walked out of the banquet hall he reflected on a wonderful career that had spanned five decades. All night people had asked him, "So, what will you do with yourself now that you're retired?" He was quick to show the picture of the beautiful motor home he and his wife had purchased and equipped for their two-year journey across the country. One morning the following week, as the sun arose, Hank got up to stretch and start his day. The stroke hit him with no warning. By the evening he was stable, alive, but his retirement plans had been radically redefined. He and his wife would be working on rehab and speech development rather than traveling and exploring the country. "Retirement" took a sudden and unexpected turn.

Tami packed her bags the day after her college graduation and started a two-thousand-mile trip across the country to an exciting summer job at a camp in the mountains. She had everything planned and scheduled.

Two months working at camp and then back home to start a career teaching somewhere near family and friends. The unexpected snuck up on her. In the first week of her short-term adventure she met the man she would eventually marry. To the shock of her family and friends, this small-town girl took a job teaching on the other side of the country, got married, started a family, and settled into a life in a place she had never dreamed of putting down roots. It was entirely unexpected!

The unexpected, along with its sorrow or joy, happens to all of us. Every day of our lives includes the opportunity for us to be pleasantly surprised with glorious good news or blindsided with the pain of bad news. This is the nature of life, both yours and mine.

TALK ABOUT IT

Tell about a time God surprised you with a renewed friendship, a great opportunity, or a much-needed breakthrough.

or

Tell about a time the unexpected was painful and hit your life like a wave you did not see coming.

> **We have not been called to control life, to endure life, or to barely make it in this life. Jesus came that we may know life and life more abundant.**

VIDEO TEACHING

As you watch the video teaching segment for session one, use the following outline to record anything that stands out to you.

Notes

When unexpected waves crash on the shore of your life

What you can expect in this *Unexpected* study

Called to an unexpected journey of faith

Life has its fair share of tragedy and hardship

Why some people do not expect to experience God's goodness

A story of heavenly blessing invades a "hopeless" life (Acts 3:1–10):

An invitation to expect more of God

The condition

The need

The lifestyle

Learning to expect God's redemption, restoration, and new beginnings

Jesus is in the business of doing glorious and unexpected things

Believe God for the unexpected

> **God is a God of redemption, restoration, and new beginnings.**

VIDEO DISCUSSION AND BIBLE STUDY

1. Tell your group members which of the following three statements comes closest to reflecting how you live your life. Then, share how your life matches up to your expectations.

   • I tend to anticipate and brace myself for hard times, difficult situations, and struggles in life.

   • I tend to expect things to go well, my life to be blessed, and my heart will be filled with joy.

   • I don't really expect things to go good or bad; I just live life and see what happens.

2. Christine shares that some people *fear* the unexpected, *avoid* the unexpected, and *ignore* the unexpected. What are some of the reasons a person would approach the unexpected in any of these three ways?

> **Fear of the unexpected often paralyzes us and stops us from stepping into the fullness of the life that God has for us.**

Read: Psalm 119:68; 2 Timothy 1:7; and John 10:10

3. Take a moment to pray and ask God to help you identify one or two good things he might want you to expect with bold faith.

_____

_____

   Share one of these with your group and let them know how they can be praying for you to grow bold in expectation of God's goodness in your life.

Read: Acts 3:1–10

4. As you read this passage, what do you learn about the beggar, his condition, and his outlook on life?

> **We were never called to live predictable lives that are naturally possible. We are called to pursue a supernatural journey of faith.**

5. The man in this story had a limitation that got in the way of him fully expecting God to work in a powerful and personal way. What is a limiting situation or condition in your life that keeps you from fully trusting God and expecting his best?

> **When God does the unexpected, he gets the glory.**

Read: Hebrews 12:1–3

6. What are ways we can fix our eyes on Jesus and lift our faces to see him, even when life is challenging?

7. When the man in Acts 3 received God's touch and healing, he jumped and praised God. What are actual ways you can become a community who "jumps and praises God" when he does the unexpected in each of your lives?

CLOSING PRAYER

Spend time in your group praying in any of the following directions:

- Thank God for the unexpected blessings you have received.
- Pray for strength to be strong and trust Jesus when unexpected pain and sorrow come crashing into your life.
- Pray for courage to follow God on whatever unexpected journey he calls you to begin.
- Invite God to use your human "limitations" to turn your eyes toward him so you can receive all he wants to give you.

> God has so much more in store for you, and instead of fearing the unexpected, avoiding the unexpected, or ignoring the unexpected, it is time to pray for, and embrace the unexpected in our lives.

BETWEEN-SESSIONS PERSONAL STUDY

MEMORIZE AND POST IT!

Commit Psalm 16:5–6 to memory:

⁵ LORD, you alone are my portion and my cup; you make my lot secure.
⁶ The boundary lines have fallen for me in pleasant places; surely I have a delightful inheritance.

Once you have done this, post it a couple of places: as a screen saver, on the door of your fridge, on the mirror in your bathroom, or another place you will see it frequently. Each time you look at this passage, unleash it in your mind and heart. Speak it aloud! Trust that he is leading you forward.

Let the truth of this Spirit-inspired declaration give you confidence and certainty that whatever unexpected event comes your way—whether good or bad—God is moving in and through your life.

> God does not always do what we want,
> when we want, or how we want, but
> he is always ready to do exceedingly
> abundantly above and beyond anything
> we could ever ask or think.

BOLD EXPECTATIONS

In the passage you studied in this session the beggar was ready to receive far less than what God wanted to give him. The beggar was expecting some loose change, but God wanted to unloose him from his life of bondage and make him whole. God wanted to bless the man!

It is time for us to expect more from God. Make a list of *five* things you believe God might want do in your life, give you, or set you free from. Then, write a brief prayer of faith and expectation for each.

— 1 —

What I am trusting and expecting God to do, provide, or deliver me from:

My faith-filled prayer of expectation . . .

— **2** —

What I am trusting and expecting God to do, provide, or deliver
me from:

My faith-filled prayer of expectation . . .

— **3** —

What I am trusting and expecting God to do, provide, or deliver
me from:

My faith-filled prayer of expectation . . .

— 4 —

What I am trusting and expecting God to do, provide, or deliver
me from:

My faith-filled prayer of expectation . . .

— 5 —

What I am trusting and expecting God to do, provide, or deliver
me from:

My faith-filled prayer of expectation . . .

Believe God for unexpected blessings.

JUMPING FOR JOY

One way we can "jump for joy" is to express to God that we are truly thankful for what he has done in our lives. When we notice his unexpected goodness and tell him so, God takes delight.

Make a list of *five to ten* things God has done for you that were good, gracious, undeserved, and unexpected. You might want to start in your childhood and think forward through the years of your life:

- _____
- _____
- _____
- _____
- _____
- _____
- _____
- _____
- _____
- _____

As you read this list, think of some way you can "jump for joy." It could be singing a song of praise, writing God a note of thanks, sharing this list with someone, or even physically jumping for joy!

> **There is no reason for grace but grace.**

What has God been teaching you through the thankfulness exercise you just completed?

> **If we allow God to, he will interrupt our lives and shatter our expected routines with his unexpected blessings.**

JOURNAL

Use the space provided to write some reflections on any of the following topics:

- What can you do to grow your confidence that God can be trusted and that his unexpected plan for you is good—even when circumstances aren't?
- What can you learn from people you know who live a bold life of trusting God?
- What are ways you can celebrate God's unexpected goodness in your life?
- How can you teach the next generation that God has good and unexpected plans for their lives?

_____

_____

_____

_____

_____

_____

_____

_____

_____

_____

_____

_____

> **Many people experience a spiritual life far less than all that God has purposed for them, primarily because they do not expect the unexpected when it comes to the things of God.**

RECOMMENDED READING

Read chapters 1 and 2 of *Unexpected* by Christine Caine to reflect more on what God is teaching you through this study.

Session Two

UNEXPECTED PEOPLE

INTRODUCTION

Have you ever noticed that when you see the same thing over and over again, you can actually stop seeing it? The carpet in your living room has a number of stains and you mean to clean them. You are embarrassed and know that they look bad. You tell yourself that you are going to get some stain remover and scrub them out. But a few weeks go by, then a few months. Before you know it, you don't even see the stains. They don't bother you because you don't notice them anymore. They have blended into the landscape of your home.

You clean the house and put a few piles of random stuff on the floor near the back door. The plan is to find a place for these things or give them away. A month later the piles are still there, but you have "forgotten" about them. They have not gone away; you just don't see them anymore.

There is something about the human mind that has the ability to stop seeing things right in front of our eyes. When we are "blind" to a stain on the carpet or a pile by the back door, it's not such a big deal. The problem is that we can do this exact thing with what God says matters most in the entire universe. We can stop seeing people—like the man who stands on the corner hoping for a few dollars, the one that we pass daily on our commute to the office.

Or the woman at church who sits in front of us at church week after week. She's faithfully there, and always alone. We're not even sure of her last name. We've not thought to go and sit beside her, to befriend her.

Or, we watch the familiar scenes of starving children depicted in a commercial that always airs during our favorite weekly TV show. They live a world away from us, but they are still people whom God loves and who desperately need help. We have seen these kinds of appeals enough times that perhaps our hearts have become calloused and our eyes blind. So, we drive on to work or turn the channel or attend church and leave with no emotional response.

How often do we go through our week looking at everything but seeing nothing? Though such behavior can be inconsequential, when it happens with a life made in the image of God and loved by our heavenly Father, it is tragic!

> **Looking and seeing are not the same thing. When you look, you can look away or over look. But when you see, you cannot un-see.**

TALK ABOUT IT

Tell about a time you looked but didn't see—when you stopped seeing a mess, something broken, or something with a big stain. Why did you stop noticing something that bothered you at first?

or

Tell of a situation about which you realize you have not been truly seeing a person or group of people in need because their presence has become so familiar that you have learned to tune them out. How do you think God feels when we become blind to the people around us who are broken, marginalized, or forgotten?

> **Sometimes we do not want to see because there is a price to seeing.**

VIDEO TEACHING

As you watch the video teaching segment for session two, use the following outline to record anything that stands out to you.

Notes

An eye-opening moment

Seeing people the way Jesus does

A rapid-fire review of the beginning of Jesus' ministry

The story of a blind Pharisee

Do we really see people?

Do we feel compassion . . . deep in our gut?

Remembering why we are here . . . we are the salt of the earth!

The fields are ripe. It is harvest time, so let's get to work!

> **Compassion is not compassion until you roll up your sleeves and go to them.**

VIDEO DISCUSSION AND BIBLE STUDY

1. Think about a time you saw something that moved you deeply with compassion and you simply could not look away. How did you respond to the feelings that God stirred in you at that moment?

   What are some of the things in our world that should evoke pain, anger, or action but have become so common that we don't really notice or respond?

2. Who are some of the groups of people that Jesus was drawn to who are often not seen or noticed in our world today? (Remember, they also were not seen or noticed in Jesus' day.) Why do you think Jesus was drawn to these people and spent so much time noticing and interacting with them?

Read: Luke 7:36–50

3. Why do you think this man was blind to what was happening right in front of him? How can some of these same attitudes and perspectives blind us today?

4. What did the woman in this story focus on and see? What did she *not* notice or seem to care about?

> **Are we expecting God to use us to reach multitudes and missing the unexpected opportunity to love, serve, or help the one right in front of us?**

Read: Luke 7:40–42

5. There is a story within this story. Jesus tells a simple but profound story to Simon the Pharisee. How is it a picture of what is unfolding at that very meal in Simon's home?

6. What are some of the attitudes and life situations that can get in the way of us seeing people the way God does?

> **If we do not see people, how will they know Jesus sees them?**

7. Simon not only missed the beauty and potential in the woman at the table, he also missed the most important and powerful person who ever walked the earth. He did not really see Jesus. What are ways we can slow down and notice the presence and hand of Jesus in our lives?

> **Without compassion, there is little sustained long-term action in any endeavor.**

8. Tell about a time you felt deep and Holy Spirit-inspired compassion for a person or group of people. What action did this lead you to take?

9. God calls all his children on mission to reach out with his love and grace. Where is the harvest ripe and ready in your life or community?

> **What is the point of our light if it is
> not penetrating the darkness?**

CLOSING PRAYER

Spend time in your group praying in any of the following directions:

- Thank God that he sees you and loves you, even though others might not see you.
- Ask God to open your eyes to see people the way Jesus sees them.
- Confess where you have failed to see people God has placed right in front of you.
- Pray for your group members to be moved by deep and lasting compassion that causes each of you to see, love, and serve those who are often missed and forgotten.

> **The church is here to take the light
> and love of Christ to dark places.**

BETWEEN-SESSIONS PERSONAL STUDY

AN EYE-OPENING DAY

Try an experiment for one twenty-four-hour period. Seek to actually see each person you encounter. As you encounter each person throughout the day, ask the following two questions and then complete the call to action.

Questions:
- How does Jesus see this person?
- How would Jesus want *me* to see this person?

Call to Action:
- Pray briefly for God's blessing on this person.

Use the space on the following pages to take note of *four or five* people who you saw in a new light when you stopped to consider how God sees them and how he would want you to view them.

Person I encountered:

How I first saw them:

How my perspective changed:

Person I encountered:

How I first saw them:

How my perspective changed:

Person I encountered:

How I first saw them:

How my perspective changed:

Person I encountered:
How I first saw them:

How my perspective changed:

Person I encountered:
How I first saw them:

How my perspective changed:

> **I have found that all of us often
> look but do not see.**

WHO AM I MISSING?

Over the next week make a point of seeking to pay attention to those who are right around you but have become so familiar that you don't really see them anymore. They could be a family member, someone at work, the person behind the counter at the local coffee shop, or anyone you see frequently. Seek to tune in to *one person* in *each* of the following locations over the coming week. Look at them more closely. Ask questions and listen. Seek to see and connect with this person on a deeper level.

Then, take note of how your relationship changes and how differently you see them by the end of the week.

Someone in your home:
How did your view of them change through the week?

Someone at your workplace or school:

How did your view of them change through the week?

Someone in your community:

How did your view of them change through the week?

Someone at your church:

How did your view of them change through the week?

> **Seeing Jesus for real ensures**
> **you see people for real.**

JESUS SIGHTINGS

Keep a list of ways you see Jesus at work by making himself known through other people and when he moves directly in your life. Keep adding to this list throughout the rest of this study.

Jesus Sighting
Where I was:

How I saw Jesus present and at work:

Jesus Sighting
Where I was:

How I saw Jesus present and at work:

Jesus Sighting

Where I was:

How I saw Jesus present and at work:

Jesus Sighting

Where I was:

How I saw Jesus present and at work:

Jesus Sighting

Where I was:

How I saw Jesus present and at work:

Jesus Sighting

Where I was:

How I saw Jesus present and at work:

Jesus Sighting

Where I was:

How I saw Jesus present and at work:

Jesus Sighting

Where I was:

How I saw Jesus present and at work:

Jesus Sighting

Where I was:

How I saw Jesus present and at work:

Jesus Sighting

Where I was:

How I saw Jesus present and at work:

> **Jesus did not come to rescue a select few good people; he came to rescue *a hurting world.***

What has God been teaching you through these "Jesus sightings"?

> **Our Christian life is not supposed to be a boring religious ritual but rather a daring adventure full of mystery, risk, faith, hope, and love.**

JOURNAL

Use the space provided to write some reflections on any of the following topics:

- How are you learning to see people you didn't notice before?
- How are you loving people you used to avoid?
- Where do you feel your eyes are still closed or blinded?
- Write a prayer asking God to open your eyes to see and your heart to feel. Then open your hands wider to serve him in a greater way.

_____

_____

_____

_____

_____

_____

_____

_____

_____

_____

If we are to reach people, then we must see people.

RECOMMENDED READING

Read chapters 3 and 4 of *Unexpected* by Christine Caine to reflect more on what God is teaching you through this study.

Session Three

AN UNEXPECTED ASSIGNMENT

INTRODUCTION

Keith was in his early fifties and ran a successful mechanic shop. He was a high school grad but had dropped out of college when he had a chance to start a business. For three decades his hard work, raw intelligence, and business sense propelled him forward until he became financially secure and respected in his community and church. Then God burst into his life and heart and called Keith to be a pastor. He had all sorts of reasons why not, but he could not deny the call. Keith sold his business, went back to school, and began serving in the church while he studied. He was in his late fifties when he was finally ordained as a pastor. If someone would have asked Keith if he was upset that God interrupted his peaceful and established life, he would have said, "I would not have it any other way . . . it has been an adventure of God-sized proportions."

Shelly was a newlywed. A schoolteacher, she was also the primary source of income because her husband was getting his Master's degree and attending school full time. Then God jumped into the middle of her plans and life. She was given a divine assignment to go back to school with her husband and prepare for what was next. By the way, God did not tell Shelly what that "next" would be, only that she was to study and get ready. Both husband and wife were in school at the same time with very little income. To top it off, she became pregnant during this challenging season. Guess what? God provided in miraculous ways; they lived very simply; and they made it through. God used Shelly's education in unexpected ways as she raised a family, served in the church, and through her studies was given opportunity to speak, write, and impact people around the world.

God is in the business of surprising us, shocking us, and stretching us! If we have the courage to follow, we will get a front-row seat to how God shows up and moves in our lives every day!

> **God is able to do unexpected things with unexpected people in unexpected places, and you could be just the person, in just the right place, to see an unexpected miracle.**

TALK ABOUT IT

Tell about a time God showed up and surprised you by calling you to do something that you never would have dreamed, chosen, or thought you could do.

or

Tell about a time you felt God call or nudge you to take a risk and follow him, but you resisted and chose to play it safe. If God were to give you a similar opportunity today, how would you respond? How would you make a different choice in light of embracing the unexpected?

> **God specializes in using unexpected people to do unexpected things for his glory.**

VIDEO TEACHING

As you watch the video teaching segment for session three, use the following outline to record anything that stands out to you.

Notes

Christine's unexpected assignment

God has good plans and an exciting assignment

An unexpected story from beginning to end (Luke 1)

We are "God carriers" to the world

God's interruptions are never convenient

The danger of fear . . . our "what ifs"

Unexpected and God-sized assignments

God interrupts our carefully planned out
life to invite us into his purpose.

VIDEO DISCUSSION AND BIBLE STUDY

1. God wants his people to bear much fruit (John 15:8). Describe the kind of legacy or impact you are leaving in *one* of the following areas:
   - On your family
   - On your church
   - On your community
   - On non-believers who are in your life

We were created on purpose for a purpose.

Read: Luke 1:26–38

2. List all that happens in Luke 1:26–38 that is unexpected:

- _____
- _____
- _____
- _____
- _____

   How do you see God using the unexpected to accomplish his will in people and in the world?

3. How does Mary respond to God's inconvenient assignment and what do you learn from her example?

> **God was not looking for Mary's ability; he was looking for her availability and willingness to say yes to her divine assignment.**

4. Tell about ways God has worked in your life and called you to do things that were inconvenient. How has God used these moments of unexpected challenge to bring glory to himself and to bless others?

> **The people God uses are NOT**
> **FEAR-LESS but FAITH-FUL.**

5. Mary would have felt unqualified and unprepared for her unexpected assignment of bringing Jesus into the world. Christine shared how she felt like she was the last person God would call for the assignments he has given her. List *two or three* things in your life, past or present, that make you feel unqualified or unprepared to step confidently into God's assignments for you.

- _____
- _____
- _____

Share one of these with your group and tell them how they can pray for you as you seek ways to overcome this barrier so that you are in a place to boldly and faithfully follow God's unexpected assignments on your life.

6. Christine says, "When we have favor, it is for God's purpose!" List *two or three* ways God has shown favor on you, blessed you, or uniquely been good to you:

- _____
- _____
- _____

Tell your group about one of these and share how you believe you could use this good gift from God for his purposes.

Favor in our lives is for God's purpose, not for self-indulgence.

7. Give an example of a recent interruption (big or small) and how you responded.

8. If God clearly interrupted you today and called you to make a major life shift, what obstacles would you need to remove to follow him fully into his divine assignment?

> **Living a life of faith is living a life of risk. It is embracing the unexpected invitations from God and saying YES. Yes to the faith journey.**

9. What are some of the "what ifs" that can rule our hearts and minds and cause us to freeze in fear rather than trust God and embrace the unexpected?

Read: 2 Corinthians 1:3–4 in unison as a group. After you have read it, read it again and think deeply about the word "comfort" and what God is teaching us in this passage.

> [3] Praise be to the God and Father of our Lord Jesus Christ, the Father of compassion and the God of all comfort, [4] who comforts us in all our troubles, so that we can comfort those in any trouble with the comfort we ourselves receive from God.

> **We have to put more faith in the promises of God than in our "what ifs."**

CLOSING PRAYER

Spend time in your group praying in any of the following directions:

- Boldly ask God to help you bear more and more fruit in your life so that he can get more and more glory.
- Pray for God to free you from fear and "what if" thinking.
- Ask the Holy Spirit to give you a heart and lips that declare "yes" quickly and confidently when he invites you into unexpected assignments.
- Thank God for the amazing favor he has shown you, and ask how he wants to bless others and bring himself glory through you.

> **No one is qualified or able to do a supernatural thing; only God can do that.**

BETWEEN-SESSIONS PERSONAL STUDY

GOD'S GLORY . . . OUR FRUIT

God is glorified when we bear fruit in our lives. He takes delight in it. Take time to focus on three areas in which God has brought fruit into the world through your life, noting examples of each. Then, celebrate with the God who celebrates with you.

Fruit through Your Words

- _____
- _____
- _____
- _____

Read a couple of these ways out loud and then lift up a prayer thanking God that he would use you to speak in ways that honor him, lift others up, and share his love with the world.

Fruit through Your Service

- _____
- _____
- _____
- _____

As you look at this list, commit to continue humbly serving God and the people he places in your life faithfully.

Fruit through Your Generosity and Sharing

- _____
- _____
- _____
- _____

Think about what you have right now that could be invested in other people's lives. Commit to share with growing joyful generosity.

> **God created us in his image, called us for his purpose, and empowers us to be fruitful on the earth.**

FACING MY "WHAT IFS"

List your three biggest fears. Then, identify the "what ifs" that are born out of these fears. Finally, come up with one Bible verse or passage that confronts this fear and one action you can take to overcome this fear.

My Fear: _____

The "what ifs" that this fear grows in my heart and mind:

A Bible verse or passage that confronts this fear:

My action commitment to help me overcome this fear and the related "what ifs":

My Fear: _____

The "what ifs" that this fear grows in my heart and mind:

A Bible verse or passage that confronts this fear:

My action commitment to help me overcome this fear and the related "what ifs":

My Fear: _____

The "what ifs" that this fear grows in my heart and mind:

A Bible verse or passage that confronts this fear:

My action commitment to help me overcome this fear and the related "what ifs":

Silence your "what ifs" by replacing what
you do not know about the future with what
you *do* know about the goodness of God.

BIG PRAYERS . . . THE "YES" OF FAITH

Write a prayer that expresses a "yes" attitude to God. Commit to saying yes to divine interruptions, yes to unexpected assignments, and yes even when you are afraid. Seek to be bolder than you have ever been.

Faith is not the absence of fear but the presence of a stronger God.

What has God been teaching when you pray these kinds of prayers?

In order to activate the miracle, you and I must say yes to God.

JOURNAL

Use the space provided to write some reflections on any of the following topics:

- What makes you feel unqualified to follow God and serve him fully? How does his Word debunk the lies in your mind and heart?
- How has God poured out his favor on you? How can you let this overflow into the lives of other people?
- What are your biggest "what ifs"? How can God set you free from these fears so that you can quickly and fully follow his unexpected assignments?

_____

_____

_____

_____

_____

_____

_____

_____

_____

_____

_____

_____

_____

Impossible is where God starts and miracles are what God does.

RECOMMENDED READING

Read chapters 5 and 6 of *Unexpected* by Christine Caine to reflect more on what God is teaching you through this study.

UNEXPECTED ENDINGS BRING NEW BEGINNINGS

INTRODUCTION

He was born in 1725 and given a simple and common name, John. His mother died when he was just seven years old. His father was a shipmaster and took John to sea for the first time at age eleven. Through a strange series of unexpected events John became a sailor . . . first in the military and then working in the slave trade.

For many years he saw nothing wrong with taking human beings, enslaving them, shipping them across the world, and selling them as if they were little more than livestock. Even after he had a conversion experience at sea during a life-threatening storm, he still worked in the slave business.

Later in life John began serving in ministry as a lay pastor and preacher and eventually as an ordained minister. As the years passed he allowed the Word of God and the conviction of the Holy Spirit to pierce his heart. John repented of his slave-trading sins and wrote a powerful paper, *Thoughts Upon the Slave Trade*, in which he told the world of the horrific conditions of the trade ships and how these people were really treated. With time he partnered with William Wilberforce and others who were battling against the slave trade.

In 1779 a hymnbook was released with some songs John had written. One of them was titled: *Faith Review and Expectation*. This hymn, written by a pastor who was a former slave trader, is still sung today and has been retitled with the opening phrase of the song. Here is the first stanza of that song:

Amazing Grace! how sweet the sound

That saved a wretch like me

I once was lost, but now am found

Was blind but now I see

—Reverend John Newton

> **God specializes in using the unexpected to do the unexpected in unexpected ways. That means you and I qualify.**

TALK ABOUT IT

God doesn't waste anything from our past. Like Reverend John Newton, Christine can see how God has taken everything in her past that the enemy meant for evil and he's turned it around. She says Joseph best summed up how she feels when he said to his brothers, *"You intended to harm me, but God intended it for good to accomplish what is now being done, the saving of many lives"* (Genesis 50:20). It is indeed her life verse.

Tell about how God has healed or redeemed something from your past and is using it for good or to help others.

> **Unexpected endings can and do bring unexpected new beginnings.**

VIDEO TEACHING

As you watch the video teaching segment for session four, use the following outline to record anything that stands out to you.

Notes

An honest look at our family history!

The end of the past and new beginnings

The story of the crucifixion . . . unexpected suffering (John 19:1–30)

The most powerful word ever spoken: *tetelestai* ("it is finished")

The most powerful point in human history . . . the cross

Grace or works?

What God has finished is truly finished!

> **Because it is finished, we can have forgiveness for our past, a brand new life for today, and a hope for the future.**

VIDEO DISCUSSION AND BIBLE STUDY

1. What is one good and helpful behavior or pattern your family passed on to you that you want to see continued for generations to come?

What is one pattern, attitude, or behavior that you want to leave in the past and *not* see impact the next generation?

Read: John 19:1–5, 28–30

2. How was Jesus hurt and abused in *each* of the following ways?

Physically

Emotionally and relationally

Spiritually

> **Jesus said, "It is finished!" He did not say, "I am finished." This was a victory shout, not an admission of defeat.**

3. When Jesus told Pilate that Pilate had no power over his life or death (John 19:11), what was he getting at? What did Jesus mean when he said, "No one takes my life from me, but I lay it down of my own accord" (John 10:18)? Why does this matter?

4. How did Jesus show compassion and care while he was being crucified and dying for our sins? (Think of how he cared for his mother, for John, for the thief on the cross, and for the world.)

5. This one word, *tetelestai*, has changed the whole world. How has the finished work of Jesus on the cross changed the course of history? How has it changed your life and home?

Tetelestai: **The tense is perfect passive indicative, which means the progress of an action is complete and the result is ongoing with full effect.**

6. On the cross Jesus won the full victory and destroyed the power of the enemy. How has the cross of Jesus and his willing sacrifice overcome and destroyed the following?

Fear of death and the grave

The power and authority of the devil

The judgment we deserved for sin

7. The work of Jesus on the cross and the power of the resurrection has graciously gifted believers with many things. Give an example of how you are experiencing one of these gifts of salvation:
  • Healing
  • Freedom
  • Life
  • Peace
  • Joy
  • Hope

Sin makes us dead and Jesus makes us alive. Jesus did not come to make bad people good, but dead people alive.

8. On the cross Jesus became the final sacrifice. No other sacrifice will ever be needed. Why is works-based religion (believing our actions and behavior can add to our salvation) so exhausting? Why is living by faith in the grace of Jesus so freeing and life-giving?

Read: Romans 3:23; 6:23; 5:8; 8:1

9. How have you come to life since placing your faith in Jesus? Where do you need to find new life, hope, and joy in Jesus? How can your group members pray for you and encourage you as you seek to find full life in Jesus?

> Because IT is finished, you are not finished. His last breath was our first. His last word was our first word. When he died, we came to life. Because IT is finished, we are not finished.

CLOSING PRAYER

Spend time in your group praying in any of the following directions:

- Thank Jesus for his final, absolute, and self-given sacrifice on the cross.
- Ask God to transform everything negative from your past and turn it into a catalyst for a life that glorifies him.
- Express gratefulness for an adventure-filled future because Jesus has already done all you need to be saved, loved, and made new.

> **Christian living is not about doing, but about believing in his finished work. It's not about what we can do for him, but about what he has already done for us.**

BETWEEN-SESSIONS PERSONAL STUDY

FAMILY HISTORY

Make a list of any bad habits, sinful patterns, and broken attitudes that have marked your family history:

- _____
- _____
- _____
- _____
- _____

Pick two of these and identify at least three ways in which you can see that Jesus has healed (or is healing) your past and leading you into his glorious future—where an unexpected ending is bringing a new beginning.

First area I can see a new beginning:

God's power to change my life and my family in the grace and power of Jesus . . .

1. _____
2. _____
3. _____

Second area I can see a new beginning:

God's power to change my life and my family in the grace and power of Jesus . . .

1. _____
2. _____
3. _____

> **Jesus' unexpected ending gave us all an unexpected new beginning.**

NEW BEGINNINGS

Purging the past and renouncing historical patterns of negativity is just the beginning. God wants to prepare you to set a new direction for the generations that follow you. Take time to identify three new patterns, behaviors, or God-honoring attitudes you want to instill in your life and family. Then, commit to one specific course of action that will begin to unleash this Holy Spirit-given vision into the life of your home and family.

First new pattern, action, or attitude:

What I will do in the coming weeks:

Second new pattern, action, or attitude:

What I will do in the coming weeks:

Third new pattern, action, or attitude:

What I will do in the coming weeks:

> **We are utterly dependent upon God in order to fulfill our God assignments.**

TETELESTAI . . . "PAID IN FULL!"

Use the space below to list *ten* attitudes, behaviors, or sinful actions you have committed at some time in your past. Don't be easy on yourself . . . be honest!

1. _____
2. _____
3. _____
4. _____
5. _____
6. _____
7. _____
8. _____
9. _____
10. _____

Once you have finished your list, read these one at a time. After you have read the first one, declare with your lips that Jesus has paid the price for this. He has set you free. He has conquered your shame. The guilt is gone! Then, write "Paid in full" or "TETELESTAI" over the sin again and again until you can't see the words.

> **Jesus' blood is the only blood
> that could pay for our sins.**

What is God teaching you through the exercise you just completed?

> **We cannot complete a completed work.
> We cannot finish a finished work. . . . How
> can anything I do ever surpass the perfect
> finished work of Christ on the cross?**

JOURNAL

Use the space provided to write some reflections on any of the following topics:

- What has God set you free from?
- What has God called you to do and be as you go forward?
- What do you hold on to that Jesus has forgotten and dealt with? How can you release this to Jesus today?

_____

_____

_____

_____

_____

_____

_____

_____

_____

_____

_____

_____

Say YES to the unexpected assignment God has for you.

RECOMMENDED READING

Read chapters 7 and 8 of *Unexpected* by Christine Caine to reflect more on what God is teaching you through this study.

UNEXPECTED RESURRECTION

INTRODUCTION

Curtis was a motivated, hardworking kid all through middle school and high school. He excelled in sports and academics and loved life. By the time he graduated from high school his parents were certain he could navigate the challenges and rigors of university. They were proud when he headed out of their home and out of state for this new chapter of his life.

Over the next two years their confidence in Curtis' ability to manage the challenges of adult life began to wane. Each time he came home he was more distant and withdrawn. With time his appearance began to change as he lost weight and looked more and more frail. They asked concerned questions, but Curtis kept his mouth and heart shut. The joyful and engaging son they had sent away to college seemed to disappear; a new person was living inside his skin. They barely recognized him.

When they found the needles and drugs in his backpack they were heartbroken, but not surprised. When confronted, Curtis did not deny the reality that he was an addict. He actually said that he loved the drugs and had no intention of stopping. For his parents it was a kind of death, a grave, a tomb. They offered their love, prayers, and all the help Curtis would accept. From a human perspective, things for their son looked hopeless.

Charity had been an extroverted, active youth. She had a sharp wit and people were drawn to her. She was compassionate too, always looking out for other kids who were excluded and marginalized. She dreamed of being a doctor or a nurse, and everyone believed she was destined for the medical profession.

A decade later her dreams were a distant memory. After a whirlwind marriage, a move across the country, the birth of her little girl Anna, and an unexpected divorce that hit her like a freight train, Charity found herself working nights at a bar to make ends meet. The money was good and she was doing all she could to support herself and her daughter. But the bar scene led her down a road she never wanted. Shame captured her heart and darkness descended on her life. Except for the few waking hours she had each day with Anna, her life felt like death, a tomb, a prison. The days she dropped her precious little girl off with her father and spent the night alone were the darkest of all. She could see no way out.

Turn the clock forward six years in each of these broken lives. The stone has been rolled away and the resurrection presence of Jesus has invaded their souls. Curtis, drug-free for almost five years, has recommitted his life to Christ and become a youth pastor at a great church. He has reconnected with his parents. To his delight, he is newly married to a bright and passionate Christian woman he met in his church's recovery group. Her name is Charity, and Charity's daughter Anna already loves him and calls him Daddy.

Charity's memories of her time working at a bar are disappearing in the rearview mirror. She is devouring online courses in nursing, working part-time in a senior citizens center (where the people absolutely love her), and delighting in the challenges of building a healthy Christian home with Curtis.

The road is not easy. Finances are tight. Time management is complex. The battle with addictions demands diligent attention, but Curtis and Charity love Jesus, each other, and Anna. They are living a life of new hope and new dreams. The stone has been rolled away! Light has replaced darkness! The resurrection power of Jesus is alive in their hearts and home. God has done what he does best . . . rolled the stone away and invited his life and light into the lives of his children!

> **Fix your eyes on Jesus and not on your past.**

TALK ABOUT IT

Tell a story about someone you know who went through a season of life that felt like a hopeless tomb. How did God roll the stone away, and how has the person's life changed?

or

Tell about a period in your life where you felt like you were trapped in a dark place. How did God roll the stone away with his resurrection power?

> **The good news of the resurrection is that nothing could hold Jesus down. Because he is alive, we can be alive in him.**

VIDEO TEACHING

As you watch the video teaching segment for session five, use the following outline to record anything that stands out to you.

Notes

An unexpected death . . . when we lose a loved one

He is risen (Mark 16:1–7)

Who will move the stone?

Facing "immovable objects"

What is "immovable" can become movable

When we look up, everything changes

The resurrection is the vindication of all our hopes

His love makes dead people alive

God's love . . . the center of the good news

When you hear good news, tell someone!

> **The good news is that what is immovable can become movable.**

> **Let Jesus move the immovable.**

VIDEO DISCUSSION AND BIBLE STUDY

1. Tell about someone you love who passed away. What did you love about that person and what do you miss?

2. In what ways does the resurrection of Jesus give us comfort and hope when we lose a loved one, go to a funeral, and stand at a graveside?

Read: Mark 16:1–7

3. In the Mark passage three women go to a grave to say goodbye to Jesus. In their minds this is a farewell trip. What happened to their *expectations*, their *hearts*, and their *lives* by the time they left the tomb?

> **We do not need a God made in our image who can only do what we do. We need a God who can roll away the stones that keep us in dark tombs.**

4. Mary, Mary, and Salome saw this trip to the tomb as an ending, a farewell, a conclusion. God turned it into a beginning, a new mission, a fresh start! Share about an experience in your life (or the life of a Christian you know) that felt like the end of the road, but God turned it into a new beginning.

5. In what area do you feel as though you have a stone blocking your way forward to the freedom, hope, and life you know God wants for you? (It could be a habit, a strained relationship, a physical limitation, an emotional challenge, a fear . . . anything that is hindering you.) How can your group members pray for you and partner with you and God to roll this stone away?

> **Impossible is where Jesus starts.**
> **Miracles are what he does.**

Read: Psalm 121

6. What attitudes and life experiences can cause us to keep our eyes turned downward, focused on the obstacles and stones in our way?

What changes when we stop looking down at all the challenges and stones blocking our way and begin looking up to see the face of Jesus and the presence of God's power in our lives? In what ways can we turn our eyes upward, focused on our Lord and leader?

Read: Ephesians 2:1–7

7. The Ephesians 2 passage opens our eyes to three profound truths. Talk about each of these:
    - *Who we were before we followed Jesus.* What is the spiritual condition and lifestyle of a person who has not entered into a life-saving relationship with Jesus?

    - *Who we are as followers of Jesus.* How does our spiritual condition change when we become children of God through faith in Jesus?

    - *How our salvation was made possible.* What has God done to make salvation and new life available to you and me?

> **Look up to the resurrected Christ—because where you look is where you will go.**

Read: Romans 5:8; John 3:16–17; 1 John 4:9–10; Galatians 2:20

8. The center of the good news is that God is love. Why must we live with a deep and personal awareness of God's love if we are going to fully understand the gospel of Jesus? How does a personal acceptance of God's love change the way we tell others about who Jesus is and what he has done for them?

> **God is not mad *at* you. He is mad *about* you. It is a crazy love.**

9. Consider one person in your life who has not yet received the love of God and embraced the free gift of salvation that Jesus offers. How can your group members pray for you (and this person) as you seek to reach out to share the story and grace of Jesus?

10. When we understand the love of God and gift of grace that Jesus offers, every aspect of our lives changes. Share one way your life has dramatically changed since the stone rolled away and you became a follower of Jesus.

> There is no stone too large. No tomb too cold. No hell too dark, that God can't move it, warm it, light it.

CLOSING PRAYER

Spend time in your group praying in any of the following directions:

- Thank God for a person he used to help you grow in faith and who is now with Jesus.
- Intercede for a person you care about who is experiencing a season that feels like a tomb. Ask the Holy Spirit to breathe hope into their life and help them turn their eyes up to Jesus.
- Thank Jesus for the stones he has rolled away to give you new life.
- Celebrate the hope that Jesus gives you every day because he is alive, present, and powerful in your life.
- Pray for a person you love and care about who has not yet encountered the resurrected Jesus and who still needs the stone rolled away in their life.

God can unexpectedly move mountains that you cannot climb.

PERSONAL STUDY
FOR THE
COMING DAYS

THE POWER OF MEMORIES

Identify one person in your life who has had a big impact on your relationship with Jesus. List five lessons they taught you, ways they showed God's love to you, or things they did to cheer you on in your faith:

- _____
- _____
- _____
- _____
- _____

Reflect on the impact this person had on your life and do three things:

First, lift up a prayer of humble thankfulness that God placed this person in your life.

Second, identify two specific ways you can pay it forward by doing the same thing for a younger Christian God has placed in your life.

- _____
- _____

Third, if this person is still living, write them a note and thank them for specific ways God has used them to shape and deepen your faith.

> **The same power that conquered the grave can live in you, rescue you, heal you, empower you, and set you free.**

LEARNING TO LOOK UP

Read Psalm 121 three or four times, slowly and reflectively. Think deeply about the invitation to look up to God and fix your focus on him.

Write a prayer of honest confession, telling God where your eyes are often focused. Think about the distractions you fixate on, the worries that consume your attention, and the earthly stuff that cries for your devotion.

Admit these to God. He knows, and he loves you. Confess these things to him.

Identify two or three specific things you can do to turn your eyes toward God in the flow of a normal day. How can you lift up your eyes to the Lord?

When you look up, you see unexpected things you never thought you would see. When you look down, you stay down.

THAT WAS THEN, THIS IS NOW

We all have walked a journey of transformation. God is in the business of rolling stones away. This means each of us have many before-and-after life snapshots. Using the following chart, think about who you were before God rolled a specific stone away and who you are becoming as you walk in the light and resurrection power of Jesus. An example has been provided.

Then	The Stone God Rolled Away	Now
I worried about everything. My mind could not rest. I found myself consumed and exhausted over things I could not control or change.	Fear and Anxiety	I come to God with my worries and give them to him in prayer. I still have moments of worry, but I feel much more peace and trust.

> **Your past does not need to define your future. Your history is not your destiny.**

What is God teaching you through the before-and-after exercise you just completed?

> **The resurrection is the vindication of all our hopes.**

JOURNAL

Use the space provided to write some reflections on any of the following topics:

- How do you want to be remembered after you die and go to be with Jesus? Who specifically do you want to have impacted for the sake of Jesus?
- Write prayers for people you care about still trapped in the tomb of sin. Cry out to God to roll the stone away and lead them out into the light of Jesus.

- Journal about how the resurrection power of Jesus has changed your attitudes and actions.

_____

_____

_____

_____

_____

_____

_____

_____

_____

_____

_____

_____

_____

_____

God does what we can never do.

He does the unexpected.

RECOMMENDED READING

Read chapters 9 and 10 of *Unexpected* by Christine Caine to reflect more on what God is teaching you through this study.

SMALL GROUP LEADER HELPS

To ensure a successful small group experience, read the following information before beginning.

GROUP PREPARATION

Whether your small group has been meeting together for years or is gathering for the first time, be sure to designate a consistent time and place to work through the five sessions. Once you establish the when and where of your times together, select a facilitator who will keep discussions on track and an eye on the clock. If you choose to rotate this responsibility, assign the five sessions to their respective facilitators up front so that group members can prepare their thoughts and questions prior to the session they are responsible for leading. Follow the same assignment procedure should your group want to serve any snacks/beverages.

A NOTE TO FACILITATORS

As facilitator, you are responsible for honoring the agreed-upon time frame of each meeting, for prompting helpful discussion among your group, and for keeping the dialogue equitable by drawing out quieter members and helping more talkative members to remember that others' insights are valued in your group.

You might find it helpful to preview each session's video teaching segment (approximately 20 minutes) and then scan the discussion questions and Bible passages that pertain to it, highlighting various questions that you want to be sure to cover during your group's meeting. Ask God in advance of your time together to guide your group's discussion, and then be sensitive to the direction he wishes to lead.

Urge participants to bring their study guide, pen, and a Bible to every gathering. Encourage them to consider buying a copy of the book *Unexpected* by Christine Caine to supplement this study.

SESSION FORMAT

Each session of the study guide includes the following group components:

- **"Introduction"**—an entrée to the session's topic, which may be read by a volunteer or summarized by the facilitator
- **"Talk About It"**—icebreaker questions that relate to the session topic and invite input from every group member
- **"Video Teaching"**—an outline of the session's video teaching segment for group members to follow along and take notes if they wish

- **"Video Discussion and Bible Study"**—video-related and Bible exploration questions that reinforce the session content and elicit personal input from every group member
- **"Closing Prayer"**—several prayer cues to guide group members in closing prayer

Additionally, in each session you will find a **"Between-Sessions Personal Study"** section (**"Personal Study for the Coming Days"** for session five) that includes a personal reflection, suggestions for personal actions, a journaling opportunity, and recommended reading from the book *Unexpected*.

Unexpected

Leave Fear Behind, Move Forward in Faith, Embrace the Adventure

Christine Caine

Is it possible to have peace in an uncertain world? To not only expect the unexpected but embrace it?

Most of us want to have life under control. But God wants us to anticipate the unexpected with a faith deeply rooted in his goodness. He wants us to know that because he is in control, we don't have to be.

In *Unexpected*, beloved author Christine Caine helps us walk into the life God has for us—unknowns and all. Using dramatic examples from her own journey, Christine offers real-life strategies and biblical inspiration to help us move from fear and worry about ourselves to hope and trust in God. As we learn new ways to manage disappointment, strengthen our hearts, and build our faith, we can enjoy a new adventure with God that is more fulfilling than any day we spend trying to anticipate what will happen next.

Stepping into our God-given destiny means stepping into the unknown, but we can embrace that calling because God knows it already. Nothing in our lives takes God by surprise. So even in the midst of personal upheaval, relational challenges, financial stresses, family transitions, career disappointments, and chaotic world affairs, we can expect God to be good and do good. What other expectation do we need to have? Listen to God's dare to trust him in every unknown of your life today.

Available in stores and online!

Unashamed

Drop the Baggage, Pick up Your Freedom, Fulfill Your Destiny

Christine Caine

Shame can take on many forms. It hides in the shadows of the most successful, confident, and high-achieving woman who struggles with balancing her work and children, as well as in the heart of the broken, abused, and downtrodden woman who has been told that she will never amount to anything. Shame hides in plain sight and can hold us back in ways we do not realize. But Christine Caine wants readers to know something: we can all be free.

"I know. I've been there," writes Christine. "I was schooled in shame. It has been my constant companion from my very earliest memories. I see shame everywhere I look in the world, including in the church. It creeps from heart to heart, growing in shadowy places, feeding on itself so that those struggling with it are too shamed to seek help from shame itself."

In *Unashamed*, Christine reveals the often-hidden consequences of shame—in her own life and the lives of so many Christian women—and invites you to join her in moving from a shame-filled to a shame-free life.

In her passionate and candid style, Christine leads you into God's Word where you will see for yourself how to believe that God is bigger than your mistakes, your inadequacies, your past, and your limitations. He is more powerful than anything you've done and stronger than anything ever done to you. You can deal with your yesterday today, so that you can move on to what God has in store for you tomorrow—a powerful purpose and destiny he wants you to fulfill.

DVD curriculum and study guide also available

Unstoppable

Now with Study Guide

Running the Race You Were Born To Win

Christine Caine

Each of us has a race to run in life. But this is a different kind of race. It's more than a competition, greater than a sporting event. It's a race with eternal implications—a sprint to destiny.

But many times in our race, we're burdened and intimidated by life's challenges along the way. The task seems too tough, the path too perilous, the race too rigorous.

What if you knew the outcome of the race before it began? What if victory was promised before the starting gun ever sounded? This truth would change the way you live your life—revolutionize the way you run your race.

Slow out of the blocks? *It's okay. Don't give up!*

Trip and fall in the first turn? *Doesn't matter. The race isn't over!*

Disheartened by an unexpected obstacle? *Keep going. You can make it!*

In *Unstoppable*, bestselling author, global evangelist, and human-trafficking activist Christine Caine enthralls us with true stories and eternal principles that inspire us to run the race of our lives, receiving the baton of faith in sync with our team, the body of Christ.

Your race is now. This is your moment. When you run with God in his divine relay, you can't lose. You're running the race you were born to win.

Available in stores and online!

Unshakeable

365 Devotions for Finding Unwavering Strength in God's Word

Christine Caine

God is bigger than your current story. Bigger than fear or shame or that voice in your head that whispers that you are not enough, too broken, or too flawed. Join him in a closer relationship—one rooted in truth and *Unshakeable*. In this yearlong daily devotional, bestselling author, speaker and activist Christine Caine encourages you to find confidence to live as the person God created you to be.

Everything in our world that can be shaken will be shaken. And yet, the Bible assures us it doesn't matter what happens politically, morally, socially, or economically in the world around us if we have Christ in us—if we have the kingdom of God within us—because his kingdom is *Unshakeable*.

Through inspiring personal stories and powerful Scriptures, Christine Caine will equip you to live boldly and courageously, fully trusting our faithful God. She will inspire you how to activate living your life on mission. Unstoppable. Undaunted. Unashamed. *Unshakeable*.

> *"All of creation will be shaken and removed, so that only unshakable things will remain."*—Hebrews 12:27 NLT

Available in stores and online!

ABOLISH SLAVERY EVERYWHERE, FOREVER.

A21.ORG   f @A21campaign   ⓘ @A21   🐦 @A21

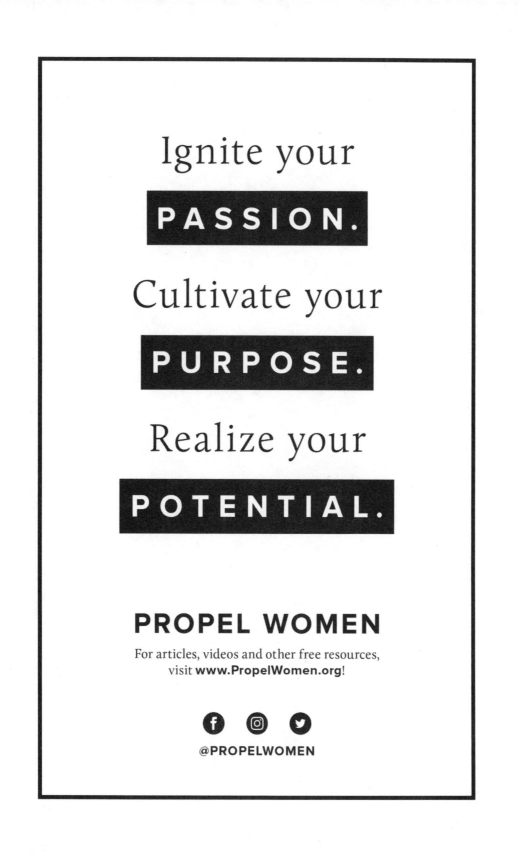